Houses can be beautiful as well as comfortable

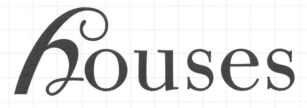

houses

Joanne Mattern

A⁺
Smart Apple Media

COPYRIGHT

❖ Published by Smart Apple Media

1980 Lookout Drive, North Mankato, MN 56003

Designed by Rita Marshall

Copyright © 2003 Smart Apple Media. International copyright reserved in
all countries. No part of this book may be reproduced in any form without
written permission from the publisher.

Printed in the United States of America

❖ Photographs by Richard Cummins, Galyn C. Hammond, JLM Visuals
(Richard P. Jacobs), Gunter Marx Photography, Tom Myers, James P. Rowan

❖ Library of Congress Cataloging-in-Publication Data

Mattern, Joanne, 1963- Houses / by Joanne Mattern. p. cm. — (Structures)

Summary: Briefly surveys the history of houses and discusses how
their design and materials may vary from place to place.

❖ ISBN 1-58340-147-4

1. Dwellings—Juvenile literature [1. Dwellings.] I. Title. II. Structures
(North Mankato, Minn.)

TH4811.5 .M38 2002   643.1—dc21   2001049968

❖ First Edition 9 8 7 6 5 4 3 2 1

CONTENTS

A Place to Call Home

It is cold and rainy outside. But inside the house it is warm and cozy. Long ago, people used caves to shelter themselves from the sun, wind, rain, and snow. Today, people live in buildings called houses. A house protects its **occupants** and keeps them comfortable. ❖ When it is hot outside, houses keep people cool. When the weather is cold and wet, houses keep people warm and dry. Houses protect people from wild animals and annoying insects. They also protect things that

This log cabin provides protection from snow

belong to the occupants, such as furniture, clothing, books, toys, and machines.

Back in Time

The first houses were built with whatever material was handy. Many of these houses were no more than stick frames covered with grass, mud, or animal hides. A hole in the roof let out smoke from fires used for cooking. ❖ Long ago, people in the southwestern part of the United States formed mud into thick bricks called adobe (ah-DOH-bee). Once the bricks were dried in the sun, they were stacked up in rows to make

walls. The Inuits, people who live near the North Pole, once

made dome-shaped houses out of snow blocks. These houses

were called igloos. ❖ When European people came to North

Grass is growing on the mud roof of this house

These houses in Burma are made of bamboo

America, they built houses out of local materials. People who settled in the northeastern forests built log cabins. People who lived on the prairies, however, found few trees. They built sod houses made of dried earth and grass.

❖ Today, most houses are built on a foundation. The foundation is made of concrete that is poured into a large

Manufactured houses are built in a factory. Then the pieces are hauled to the building site on trucks and put together.

hole in the ground. Wooden **beams** anchored in the concrete form the house's frame. The frame is then covered with wood, brick, **vinyl**, or metal.

It Takes All Kinds

For many reasons, houses look different in different

parts of the world. About 1,000 years ago, there were many

Many modern houses are built with a wooden frame

13

groups fighting wars in Europe. Rich people built castles, or fortresses, to protect themselves from enemies. Castles were built on land that was easy to defend, such as rocky hills, river bends, or islands. The ground floor of a castle was often a prison. Soldiers lived on the second floor. The lord of the castle and his family had apartments on the third floor. Although castles were large and often beautiful, most were also damp and uncomfortable to live in. ❖ Sometimes, the **climate** helps

Long ago, cows, pigs, and other animals lived in houses with people. Today, farm animals live in barns. But many people keep pets in their houses.

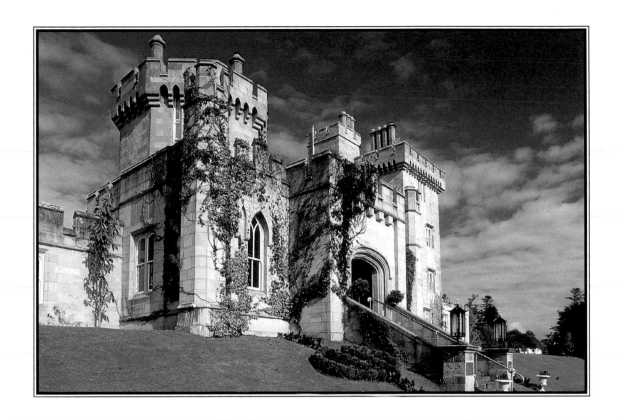

determine the kinds of houses people build. In hot climates,

one-story houses let heat rise up and out. Thick walls keep hot

air out and cool air in. Houses in snowy climates often have

The lord of this castle could see his enemies coming

steep roofs. These roofs let the snow slide off. In wet, steamy lands, houses are often built on **stilts** near the river. Even if the water rises, the houses stay dry. ❖ In Thailand, there is little open land available. So some people live on the River Kok in reed-and-bamboo houseboats—houses that float on water. Land is also hard to come by in large cities such as New York and Hong Kong. Many families in big cities live in their own apartments in

About 200 A.D., wealthy Romans built big, fancy houses. A fountain in the center court-yard helped to keep the houses cool.

This house in Peru will stay dry during a flood

apartment houses. These large buildings let a lot of people live

in a small area.

Houses of the Future

In the future, more houses will probably be built of foam,

steel, concrete, or plastic. Houses may use solar power (energy

from the sun). Special sheets called solar panels will gather

energy from the sun to heat water and power machines inside

the houses. ❖ Houses of the future will also probably be

controlled more and more by computers. In fact, some houses

already have computer equipment that can tell a person if the

milk in the refrigerator is spoiled or if there is water in the

basement. Someday, computers may even cook food for people

while they are gone. Imagine coming home from work or

school to find a hot meal waiting for you! ❖ For tens of thousands of years, people have lived in houses made of rock, wood, grass, and mud. Whatever form houses of the future take, and whatever technology they use, one thing is for sure: a house will always be a place to gather, relax, and feel safe. A house will always be a place to call home.

Long ago, most houses were round. Rectangular houses were first built in Mesopotamia, a region that is now part of Iraq.

Many houses have decorative wooden trim

Build a Model Tepee

Many Native American tribes lived in tepees. Here is how to build a model tepee of your own.

What You Need

A brown paper grocery bag

A dinner plate

Crayons or markers

Glue

Scissors

A drinking straw

What You Do

1. Cut open the grocery bag so you have one flat piece.
2. Draw a circle by tracing a dinner plate on the paper.
3. Cut out the circle, then cut it in half.
4. Use the crayons or markers to decorate one of the half-circles. You can draw shapes or pictures.
5. Bend the half-circle into a cone by gluing the straight edges together.
6. Cut off the very top of the cone to make a small opening.
7. Make a door by cutting a slit about halfway up one side of the cone and folding the paper back.
8. Stick a drinking straw into the top hole to hold the tepee up.

A tepee made of cloth stretched over a stick frame

Index

Words to Know

beams (BEEMZ)—long, thick pieces of wood

climate (KLY-mit)—the weather that is usually found in a certain place

manufactured (man-yoo-FAK-shurd)—made by hand or by machines

occupants (OCK-yoo-puntz)—people who live in a building

stilts (STILTS)—wooden poles that stand upright and hold a building above the ground or water

vinyl (VY-nuhl)—a hard and durable plastic-like material

Read More

Ashman, Linda. *Castles, Caves, and Honeycombs*. San Diego: Harcourt, 2001.

Collins, Carolyn Strom. *Inside Laura's Little House*. New York: HarperCollins, 2000.

Gibbons, Gail. *How a House Is Built*. New York: Holiday House, 1996.

Kalman, Bobbie. *Homes Around the World*. New York: Crabtree Publishing, 1994.

Internet Sites

Houses and Homes
http://www.schools.ash.org.au/elanorah/homes.htm

How House Construction Works
http://www.howstuffworks.com/house.htm

I N F O R M A T I O N